To:

From:

SEAFOOD AND FISH
delicious recipes

Printed in the United States of America

ISBN 1-56383-023-X

TABLE OF CONTENTS

APPETIZERS

CRAB SPREAD

1-7 oz. can crabmeat
1-8 oz. jar shrimp sauce

1-8 oz. cream cheese
Crackers

Combine drained and flaked crabmeat with shrimp sauce. Pour this mixture over the block of cream cheese and serve as a spread with crackers.

HOT CRAB DIP

1-8 oz. pkg. cream cheese
½ C. mayonnaise
2 green onions, sliced
1 T. dried parsley flakes

1-6 oz. can crabmeat,
  drained and flaked
½ C. slivered almonds
2 T. dry white wine
1 T. horseradish
¼ tsp. Worcestershire sauce

Place cream cheese in medium glass mixing bowl. Microwave about 2 to 2½ minutes on Medium-High (Roast) or until soft. Add all ingredients and microwave 4 to 6 minutes on Medium-High (Roast) or until hot (about 120° F.). Serve with crackers. Makes 2 cups.

CRAB SNACK

8 oz. cream cheese,
  softened
1 T. horseradish

1 C. ketchup
1-6 oz. crabmeat

Spread softened cheese in round 8" pan. Mix 1 cup ketchup and 1 tablespoon horseradish. Spread on top of cheese. Sprinkle with drained crabmeat. Cool. Serve with crackers.

CRAB TRIANGLES

1-6 to 8 oz. pkg. frozen
  crabmeat, thawed
2 T. butter
¼ C. green onions, sliced
1 C. chopped mushrooms
1 C. shredded Monterey
  Jack cheese

1-3 oz. pkg. cream cheese,
  softened
⅓ C. mayonnaise
2 T. chopped fresh parsley
¼ lb. phyllo pastry sheets
½ C. melted butter

Drain and slice crab. Melt butter; add onions and saute 1 minute. Add mushrooms and saute 1 minute longer. Combine with crab, cheeses, mayonnaise and parsley. Spread phyllo sheets out in layers, making 2 layers at a time. (Keep unused phyllo covered with a clean damp towel to prevent drying out.) Cut each group of 2 into strips approximately 2x10". Brush each strip with melted butter. Spoon a scant tablespoon of filing onto each end of row. Fold pastry over filling to form a triangle. Continue folding into triangles, as you would a flag, the length of the strip. Seal seam with butter. AT THIS POINT, THE APPETIZERS CAN BE WRAPPED IN FREEZER PAPER AND FROZEN. Place seam side down on a greased baking sheet. Bake at 350° for 30 minutes or until crisp and golden. Serve hot. Makes about 3 dozen.

CRABMEAT RAREBIT

3 T. flour
3 T. butter
2 T. ketchup
1 large or 2 small cans
  crabmeat
Paprika

3 C. milk
3 eggs
2 T. Worcestershire sauce
1 lb. American cheese,
  cut up
Holland rusks

Melt butter in double boiler, blend in flour, add milk (more if too thick). Stir in cheese and when it is all melted, stir in eggs which have been slightly beaten with seasonings. Add crabmeat. Serve in chafing dish or fondue pot with Holland rusks or your favorite bread cubes.
NOTE: Crabmeat may be substituted with lobster or shrimp.

JALAPENO SHRIMPIES

1 jar jalapenos

1-6 oz. pkg. cream cheese
1 can medium shrimp

Drain and rinse jalapenos. Slice in half lengthwise. Fill peppers with cream cheese and top each one with one shrimp. Refrigerate until serving time.

SHRIMP DIP

1-8 oz. pkg. soft cream
  cheese
1-6½ oz. can tiny shrimp
1 T. real mayonnaise

1 tsp. lemon juice
1 tsp. Worcestershire sauce
1 tsp. garlic powder

Thoroughly blend all ingredients. Keep refrigerated in closed container. Will keep up to 1 month in refrigerator. Serve with crisp crackers or vegetables. If blender or mixer is used, it will shred the shrimp more easily.

SHRIMP SPREAD

2-8 oz. pkgs. cream cheese
1-12 oz. bottle shrimp sauce
(commercial sauce can be
used or you can make your
own)

1-6 oz. pkg. precooked,
frozen miniature shrimp,
thawed

Place cream cheese, end to end, in shallow dish. Combine shrimp and shrimp sauce. Pour over cream cheese. Serve with crackers.

9

SHRIMP BALL

2-6 or 8 oz. pkgs. small
    frozen, cooked shrimp
2-8 oz. pkgs. cream cheese,
    softened
1 tsp. minced onion
¼ tsp. garlic salt

½ to 1 tsp. hot sauce (to
    taste)
Mayonnaise to moisten
    (about 2 T.)
Salt to taste
Chopped parsley (dried or
    fresh)

Thaw and drain shrimp <u>well</u> (may press in paper towels to remove all water). Combine cream cheese, onion, garlic salt, hot sauce, mayonnaise and salt (if needed). Add shrimp and mix well. Form into a ball; wrap in plastic wrap. Chill until ready to serve. Sprinkle with chopped parsley. Serve with assorted crackers. Make a day ahead so flavors will blend. Makes 1 ball (serves approximately 50).

TIPS FOR GARNISH: Instead of sprinkling with chopped parsley, top ball with shrimp and garnish base with fresh parsley. For Christmas, sprinkle ball with parsley and paprika.

SHRIMP PATÉ

1 can tomato soup,
  undiluted
1-8 oz. pkg. cream cheese
1½ T. unflavored gelatin

1 C. mayonnaise
¾ C. finely chopped celery
¾ C. finely chopped green
  onions
1 can shrimp, chopped

Heat soup to boiling point, add cream cheese and stir until melted. (Watch scorching.) Add mayonnaise, celery, onions and shrimp. Stir well. Soften gelatin in ¼ cup cold water, add to mix. Pour into oiled 2-quart mold. Chill overnight. Soup and cream cheese will scorch if you do not stir constantly. Serves 10 to 15.

SHRIMP BUTTER

2-5 oz. cans small shrimp,
   drained or cooked,
   chopped
1 T. minced onion
3 T. lemon juice

4 T. mayonnaise
1½ sticks soft butter
8 oz. pkg. cream cheese,
   softened
Salt to taste

Combine all ingredients except shrimp; mix well (use mixer). Add shrimp. Shape in mound. Serve with crackers or party rye bread. May spread on small circles of bread, dusting the edges with minced parsley.

CLAM BOAT DIP

8 oz. herb and spice cream
   cheese
8 oz. Philadelphia cream
   cheese
3 cans minced clams (save
   juice of 1 can)
1 lemon, squeezed or 2 to
   3 T. lemon juice

¼ C. dried parsley
½ C. chopped, dried onion
2 T. Worcestershire sauce
3 drops Tabasco sauce
Salt and pepper to taste
1 loaf Italian bread, uncut
   (round or oblong)

Mix all ingredients except bread until cream cheese is blended with the rest. Add the reserved clam juice. Cut off the top of the bread and set aside. Remove the bread inside the bottom portion to leave a shell or "boat". (Save bread for "dipping".) Put cream cheese mixture in bread boat. Put lid on and wrap in foil. Bake at 350° for 3 hours. Be careful when removing from oven and opening foil, the steam makes it very hot. Serve on a tray with the bread from the inside cut in cubes around it. An additional loaf of bread can be cut up for dipping or crackers and raw vegetables can be used. The best part is eating the "boat" itself!

TUNA PATÉ

1-8 oz. pkg. cream cheese,
    softened
2 T. chili sauce or ketchup
2 T. snipped parsley
1 tsp. instant onion or 1 T.
    fresh onion

Fresh onions
1/4 tsp. hot pepper sauce
Few drops Worcestershire
    sauce
2-7 oz. cans tuna, drained

Blend all ingredients thoroughly. Form into a large mound or 2 small mounds on plate. Serve with crackers.

SOUPS, STEWS & GUMBOS

CRAB BISQUE

2 T. minced onion
2 T. butter
3 T. flour
White pepper
½ C. dry white wine

½ to ¾ lb. crabmeat
2 C. cream
1-8 oz. tomato sauce
Paprika

In medium saucepan, cook onion and butter until tender. Add flour gradually. Add wine and blend well. Cook and stir in cream; when thickened, add crab and tomato sauce. Heat thoroughly. Garnish with paprika. Do not boil. Refrigerate leftovers.

CLAM CHOWDER

10 oz. minced clams
¼ C. sliced leek
¼ C. minced onion
¼ C. finely diced green
   pepper
¼ C. finely diced celery
2 T. butter
½ C. finely diced potato
Dash pepper

1 C. heavy cream
1¾ C. milk
3 T. flour
½ tsp. Worcestershire sauce
½ tsp. Accent or seasoned
   salt
½ tsp. salt
3 drops Tabasco sauce
⅛ tsp. thyme

Heat 2 tablespoons butter in large Dutch oven, add leeks, onions, green pepper and celery; cook slowly 6 to 8 minutes or until partially tender. Scald cream and milk. Blend 3 tablespoons flour into leek mixture; cook slowly 3 minutes. Add slowly to the vegetable mix, the liquid from minced clams, the scalded milk and cream, the potatoes, Worcestershire sauce, Accent, salt, Tabasco sauce, thyme and pepper. Bring just to a boil, reduce heat and cook slowly 35 to 40 minutes. Stir often. Add minced clams and cook 5 minutes longer. Serve in bowls and sprinkle chopped parsley on each serving. (Will curdle if boiled!) Serves 4 to 6.

CREOLE FISH GUMBO

1 large onion, chopped
½ green pepper, chopped
1 clove garlic, minced
2 T. vegetable oil
2 T. flour
1-15 oz. can stewed
  tomatoes
1-6 can tomato paste
1 tsp. salt

½ tsp. chili powder
1 bay leaf
½ tsp. basil
1-10 oz. pkg. okra, sliced
  (optional)
1 T. Worcestershire sauce
1½ lbs. haddock or cod
3 C. water
3 C. cooked rice

20

Saute vegetables slightly in large pot. Stir in flour, blend well. Add remaining ingredients except fish, okra and rice. Simmer, covered, 30 minutes. Remove bay leaf. Add fish and okra. Cover and simmer additional 10 to 15 minutes or until okra is tender. Serve in soup bowls over hot, cooked rice. Serves 6 to 8.

SALMON CHOWDER

1 can salmon
3 C. water
3 medium potatoes,
  peeled and diced
3 or 4 carrots, peeled and
  diced
4 slices bacon, diced

1 C. celery, diced
1 medium onion, diced
3 T. butter
1¾ C. half and half
Salt and pepper to taste
Parsley, optional

Remove skin and bones from salmon, and crumble; set aside. Peel and dice potatoes and carrots, and put in the 3 cups water; cook until tender. DO NOT DRAIN potatoes and carrots when they are cooked. Fry bacon in skillet until crispy and brown. Remove and drain. Put celery and onion in bacon grease, and saute until tender but not brown. Remove and drain. Add celery and bacon to vegetables and water. Add the butter, half and half, salt, pepper, parsley and salmon, and heat just until heated through. DO NOT BOIL.

SHRIMP JAMBALAYA

3 large onions, chopped
2 cloves garlic, minced
½ C. green pepper, diced
1 C. uncooked rice
½ tsp. red pepper
¼ C. parsley, chopped

3 T. oil
½ C. celery, diced
2 C. shrimp, peeled
2 C. broth or water
1 tsp. salt
½ C. cut green onion tops

Brown onion in oil until deep, dark brown. Add broth or water, then celery, green pepper and garlic. Let simmer together until all are softened. Add shrimp and cook 5 minutes. Add seasonings and the rice. Cover and heat to boiling, lower heat and simmer, covered about 20 minutes. Stir very carefully, <u>once</u>, reduce heat as low as possible and steam 30 minutes. Add parsley and green onion tops before serving.

SHRIMP CHOWDER

2 T. butter or margarine
1½ lbs. shrimp, cut up fine
2 lbs. potatoes, diced
3 large onions, sliced

3 T. bacon fat
2 T. vinegar
1 small can evaporated milk
2 T. cornmeal

Cook potatoes, onions, bacon fat and vinegar with just enough water to barely cover. Just as soon as potatoes start getting soft, add shrimp and cornmeal until shrimp are well done. Serves 4.

TURTLE SOUP

1½ to 2 lbs. turtle meat,
  cooked
2 qts. chicken stock,
  strained
1 onion, diced

3 T. oil
1 T. chopped parsley
5 thin slices of lemon
Salt and pepper to taste

Brown turtle in oil. Add chopped onions and saute until just tender, not brown. Add turtle, onion, salt and pepper to hot chicken stock, heat to boiling, add parsley and simmer for 20 minutes. Serve hot with a thin slice of lemon in each bowl floating on top.

TURTLE STEW

1 turtle, cut in pieces
1 large onion, cut up
1 tsp. mixed pickling spices,
  tied in bag

½ tsp. vinegar
3 T. flour
2½ C. milk

Combine all ingredients in large kettle except flour and milk. Fill kettle with as much water as you'll want for soup and enough to cover the turtle. Cover and boil until tender, will take a couple of hours. Pour through a strainer and put juice and meat back in kettle. Take spice bag out after cooking with turtle 1 hour. Make a thickening of flour and 1 cup of milk. Add to turtle and juice slowly and add rest of milk. Heat through but do not boil.

OYSTER STEW

2 qts. whole milk
1 pt. fresh oysters

¼ C. margarine or butter
1½ tsp. salt
Dash of pepper

Melt margarine, then add oysters and saute in 4-quart heavy pan. Heat milk and add hot oysters. Oysters and milk should both be hot when combining to prevent curdling. Add salt and pepper. Stir. Simmer, but do not boil, for several hours before serving. Serves 4 to 6.

SEAFOOD GUMBO

1½ C. flour	1 bay leaf
1½ C. cooking oil	1 small can tomato paste
1 C. onion	2 lbs. fresh shrimp
½ C. bell pepper	1 can crabmeat
2 cloves garlic	Salt, pepper, cayenne
1 C. celery	pepper, to taste
1½ qts. water	1 pt. oysters and liquid

Make roux with the flour and cooking oil. Cook in iron skillet on low heat until dark brown, stirring constantly. Chop the onion, bell pepper, garlic and celery. Add to roux and saute. Pour into large pot. Add water, bay leaf, tomato paste, fresh shrimp and crabmeat. Add salt, pepper and cayenne pepper to suit taste. Simmer 30 minutes. Add oysters and liquid. Cook until shrimp are done. Serve over cooked rice. Freezes well. Recipe is better made one day ahead of time.

29

CAKES, PATTIES & LOAVES

CRAB CAKES

1 C. crabmeat
1 tsp. salad dressing
½ C. flour

1 egg, beaten
½ tsp. salt
¾ tsp. baking powder

Mix crabmeat, salad dressing and egg. Mix flour with baking powder and salt. Combine flour mixture with meat mixture. Form into patties and brown in hot grease. Serves 6.

HALIBUT LOAF

4 oz. cooked halibut
Dash of seafood seasoning
1 T. chopped parsley
1 tsp. onion flakes
¼ C. water
1 slice bread

Salt and pepper
1 tsp. lemon juice
2 T. diced celery
1 chicken bouillon cube
½ C. evaporated skim milk

Simmer parsley, onion flakes and celery in bouillon until dry. Put halibut, seasonings and lemon juice in bowl. Mince halibut mixture, add vegetables and mix. In blender, blend bread and milk until smooth. Pour over halibut. Mix thoroughly. Form into loaf and place on aluminum foil. Top with paprika before baking. Bake at 350° for 30 minutes. Bake in pan, cut into serving portions, wrap and freeze. May increase, if desired.

SALMON FRITTERS

1 C. sifted flour
1½ tsp. baking powder
½ tsp. salt
1 egg, well beaten

¼ C. finely chopped onions
1 large can of salmon
½ C. cornmeal

Mix flour, baking powder, salt and cornmeal. Next, add onions, egg and salmon. Mix well and shape into patties and fry in hot oil until golden brown. Makes about 12 large patties.

SALMON LOAF

1 can salmon, well flaked
⅔ C. milk
1½ C. crushed cracker
  or bread crumbs

2 T. melted butter
Salt and pepper to taste

Mix the above ingredients well and form into loaf shape. Place in casserole and bake in hot oven for ½ hour or until done.

SALMON CROQUETTES

1 pkg. saltine crackers
2 eggs

1 medium onion, chopped
  fine
1-16 oz. can salmon (better
  cold)

Crush crackers and mix all ingredients together. Shape and refrigerate until needed. Deep-fry.

36

SALMON PATTIES

1-15½ oz. can pink salmon   ½ C. flour
1 egg   1½ tsp. baking powder

Drain salmon; set aside 2 tablespoons of the juice. Mix salmon and egg until sticky. Stir in flour. Add baking powder to salmon juice; stir into salmon mixture. Form into small patties and fry until golden brown in hot shortening (about 5 minutes).

SALMON BALLS

2-16 oz. cans salmon
2 eggs
1½ C. liquid (salmon
  liquid plus milk)
3 C. finely crushed cracker
  crumbs
2 T. lemon juice
1 T. finely chopped onion

¼ tsp. salt
¼ tsp. lemon-pepper
½ C. diced celery
Finely crushed corn flake
  crumbs
1 can cream of mushroom
  soup
½ C. milk
½ C. grated Cheddar
  cheese

Beat eggs; add liquid. Stir in crumbs, lemon juice, onion, salt, pepper and celery. Fold in flaked salmon from which skin has been removed. Shape into small balls and roll in finely crushed cornflake crumbs. Brown in cooking oil in skillet, turning gently. Place browned balls in 2-quart casserole. Combine soup and milk, and pour over balls; sprinkle Cheddar cheese on top. Bake at 350° for 20 to 30 minutes. Serves 8 to 10.

TUNA PATTIES

2-7 oz. cans tuna,
  drained and flaked
27 sqs. saltine crackers,
  crushed
1 T. Worcestershire sauce
⅛ tsp. bottled hot pepper
  sauce (optional)

2 T. chopped parsley
  (optional)
1 egg
2 tsp. prepared mustard
3 T. mayonnaise
¼ C. margarine
Lemon wedges

Combine first 8 ingredients. Shape into 8 patties. Melt the margarine in a skillet and brown patties on both sides. Serve with lemon wedges. Makes 8-2½" patties.

LOW-CALORIE BAKED TUNA FISH CAKES

4 oz. tuna, drained
¼ tsp. dehydrated onion
 flakes
¼ C. tomato juice

Salt and pepper to taste
2 T. chopped celery
1 T. Worcestershire
1 tsp. prepared mustard

Combine all ingredients and form into 2 patties. Bake at 350° in a non-stick pan about 30 minutes. Serves 1.

CLAM FRITTERS

1 pt. clams, chopped
1 egg, beaten
Bisquick

½ C. buttermilk
Salt and pepper to taste
Hot oil for frying

Combine clams and egg; add buttermilk and enough Bisquick to make the consistency of pancake batter. Drop by spoonfuls into hot oil in frying pan. Cook like pancakes. Serves 6.

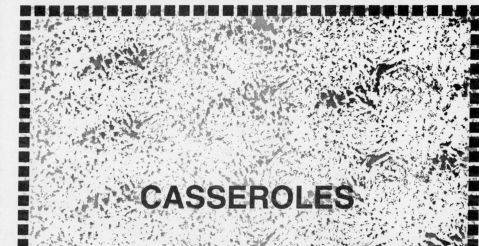

CASSEROLES

CLAM LINGUINE

3 cans whole baby clams
1 pkg. linguine
3 T. margarine
6 scallions, chopped
Salt (sparingly))

1 large bell pepper
½ lemon
1 clove garlic, chopped
Pepper to taste
Parsley, chopped

Heat olive oil in medium saucepan; add 1 tablespoon margarine and saute onion and bell pepper until tender. Add clams with some juice, garlic, lemon and margarine, pepper and continue cooking over low heat for 10 minutes. Prepare linguine according to package directions. Place linguine in oblong casserole dish and top with clam sauce and parsley. Serves 6.

WHITE CLAM SAUCE

1 stick butter
¼ C. oil
Pinch tarragon or basil
4 or 5 fresh cloves of garlic

1-10 oz. can baby clams,
* with juice*
½ pt. heavy cream
¾ C. parsley, fresh
⅔ C. Parmesan cheese
1 lb. pasta

Melt butter, add oil, tarragon or basil and peeled garlic. Simmer gently for 5 minutes. Add whole clams with juice, add cream, stir. Cook pasta, noodles or fettuccine. Drain. While hot, add Parmesan cheese and parsley and mix, tossing lightly. The cheese will melt. Pour clam sauce on and enjoy. Serve with salad. Serves 4.

CLAM DIGGER'S CASSEROLE

2-7½ oz. cans minced clams
30 saltine crackers, crushed
2 eggs

1 C. milk
1 can cream of mushroom
  soup
½ C. butter or margarine

Beat eggs. Mix all ingredients. Bake at 350° for 1 hour in casserole dish. May substitute clam juice for part of the milk. Serves 6.

CRABMEAT CASSEROLE

1 C. chopped onion	2 cans crabmeat
1 C. chopped bell pepper	1 C. bread crumbs
1 C. chopped celery	1 C. mayonnaise

Mix all ingredients, saving a few bread crumbs to sprinkle on top of casserole. Bake at 325° for 45 minutes.

CRABMEAT ROYALE

1 lb. crabmeat
1-4 oz. can mushrooms,
  drained
1 T. onion, chopped
1 tsp. Worcestershire sauce

¼ C. dry sherry (optional)
3 T. flour
1 C. milk
Salt and pepper to taste

Remove any shell from crabmeat. Saute drained mushrooms in butter for about 5 minutes. Add onion and cook until onion is tender. Add crabmeat, Worcestershire sauce and sherry, if desired. Make paste of flour and milk. Add to crabmeat mixture and cook until sauce thickens. Add salt and pepper. Spoon mixture into 1½-quart baking dish or individual shells or ramekins. Sprinkle shredded cheese over the top. Bake at 350° for 5 or 10 minutes or until cheese melts and the mixture is bubbly. Serves 6.

CRAB SUPREME

8 slices bread
1 lb. crabmeat
1 onion, chopped
½ C. mayonnaise
½ to 1 C. celery, chopped

1 can mushroom soup
½ to 1 lb. sharp cheese, grated
½ to 1 C. green pepper
4 eggs, beaten
3 C. milk

Cook celery, onion, and green pepper for 10 minutes. Drain. Dice bread (half) into 14x10x3" baking dish. Mix crabmeat, onion, mayonnaise, green pepper and celery. Spread over bread. Dice remaining 4 slices of bread and spread over crab mixture. Mix eggs and milk together and pour over the ingredients. Cover and place in refrigerator overnight. Bake at 350° for 15 minutes. Remove from oven and spoon soup over top. Sprinkle cheese and paprika over top. Bake 1 hour more until golden brown. Can be baked at 325 or 350°. Best baked in uncovered pan or Pyrex dish. Serves 8.

DEVILED CRAB

13 to 16 oz. fresh crabmeat
(pick over carefully to
remove shell or
membrane)
4 T. butter
2 T. flour
1 T. parsley
2 tsp. lemon juice

1 tsp. mustard
1 tsp. horseradish
1 tsp. salt
2 hard-cooked eggs, minced
½ C. bread crumbs
2 T. melted butter
1 C. milk

Melt the 4 tablespoons butter; stir in flour, then add parsley, lemon juice, mustard, horseradish, salt and milk. Heat, stirring until thickened. Add crabmeat and minced eggs. Fill shells or ramekins, sprinkle with the combined bread crumbs and butter. Bake at 400° for 15 minutes. Serves 6.

ROLLED FISH CASSEROLE

2½ to 3 lbs. flounder fillet
10 pieces white bread, dry
  cubes
1 onion ("hand ball" size),
  fried

1 can cream of mushroom
  soup
½ C. sour cream
¼ C. mayonnaise
¼ C. lemon juice

Soak bread in water and mix with fried onions. Use this as stuffing and roll the fish fillets with this inside. Place rolled fish in casserole dish. Mix the soup, sour cream, mayonnaise and lemon juice and pour over fish. Cook at 350° for H hour covered, 10 minutes uncovered. (Can be frozen.) Use toothpicks to keep fish rolled. Remove before serving. Serves 6 to 8.

OYSTER CASSEROLE

⅔ C. minced onions
6 T. butter, unsalted
3 T. flour
4 cans oyster stew
1 pt. oysters

2 boxes Uncle Ben's wild
  long grained rice
6 hard-boiled eggs
1½ to 2 C. unsalted cracker
  crumbs
4 T. melted butter

Cook rice according to directions and set aside. Saute onions and 6 tablespoons butter. Thicken with flour. Pour in stew and oysters. Cook until thick. Place a layer of rice, then a layer of sliced eggs in 2 large, long Pyrex dishes. Pour oyster mix over. Mix crumbs with melted butter and sprinkle over top of mixture. Dot with butter. Bake at 350° for 35 to 40 minutes. This recipe makes 2 large casseroles. It may be halved for regular casserole. Serves 16.

OYSTERS AU GRATIN

1 pt. oysters	1 tsp. prepared mustard
6 slices buttered bread	1½ tsp. paprika
2 eggs, beaten	½ C. milk
1 tsp. salt	1 C. grated cheese

Preheat oven to 350°. Trim crusts from bread. Cut each slice into quarters. Combine beaten eggs, seasonings and milk. Arrange layer of bread in buttered casserole, cover with layer of oysters. Sprinkle with grated cheese. Repeat layer, pour milk mixture over contents of dish and cover with grated cheese. Place casserole in pan of hot water, bake in moderate oven, 350° F. for 30 minutes or until brown. Serves 6.

SALMON SOUFFLE

1 stalk celery, diced
1 onion, diced
1-1 lb. can salmon, drained
¼ C. milk
⅓ C. mayonnaise
3 egg yolks

3 egg whites
1 T. bread crumbs or flour
1 T. onion soup mix
Onion or garlic powder
Dill weed

Saute celery and onion until clear. Add salmon, milk, mayonnaise, egg yolks, bread crumbs, onion soup mix, garlic or onion powder and dill weed. Mix well. Beat egg whites until stiff. Fold egg whites into salmon mixture. Pour into greased 1½-quart casserole. Bake at 350° for 1 hour.

CHARTREUSE OF SALMON

1 C. boiled salmon, minced
¼ C. cracker crumbs
Dash of cayenne
½ tsp. salt

½ level tsp. mustard
Juice of ½ lemon
2 eggs

Put salmon in a bowl; add salt, cayenne, mustard, lemon juice and cracker crumbs, moisten with the yolks of eggs. When thoroughly mixed, fold in stiffly-beaten whites. If the fish is very dry, add 2 tablespoons of milk or cream. Put into buttered ramekins or custard cups. Set them in a pan of hot water and bake 20 minutes in moderate oven (375°). Serve with hollandaise or white sauce.

SHRIMP ARTICHOKE CASSEROLE

#2 can artichoke hearts
¾ lb. cooked shrimp
¼ lb. fresh mushrooms
1½ C. cream sauce

2 T. butter
1 T. Worcestershire sauce
¼ C. dry sherry
¼ C. grated Parmesan
  cheese
Salt, pepper and paprika

Arrange artichoke hearts in buttered 1½-quart baking dish; spread shrimp over artichokes. Slice mushrooms and saute in butter for 6 minutes, add to baking dish. Mix Worcestershire sauce with sherry and cream sauce and add to baking dish. Sprinkle top with cheese and paprika. Bake at 375° for 30 to 40 minutes. Serve hot and garnish with parsley. Serves 4 to 5.

DOUBLE SHRIMP CASSEROLE

1¾ C. small shells
1 can condensed cream of
  shrimp soup
¾ C. milk
½ C. mayonnaise

1 T. chopped green onion
¼ tsp. salt
⅓ C. shredded Cheddar
  cheese
1 C. cooked shrimp
  (or 1-6 oz. can)

Cook shells according to package directions. Combine soup, milk, mayonnaise, onion and salt. Mix well. Stir in cheese, shrimp and cooked shells. Pour into 1½-quart casserole. Optional: Sprinkle with additional cheese and some fine bread crumbs. Bake, uncovered, at 350° for 30 to 35 minutes. Serves 5.

CURRIED SHRIMP WITH BROWN RICE

6 T. butter
6 T. flour
2 C. milk
2 tsp. curry powder

2 C. canned or cooked fresh
 shrimp
1½ T. chopped parsley
2 tsp. lemon juice
Boiled brown rice.

Melt butter and stir in flour to form a smooth paste. Add milk and cook over boiling water until thickened. Season with salt and curry powder, add 1 tablespoon parsley, lemon juice and shrimp, reserving a few for garnish; heat thoroughly. Line sides of 1½-quart casserole with boiled brown rice and fill center with curried shrimp, garnishing with reserved shrimp and the remaining parsley. Serves 6.

59

CHEESE SHRIMP CASSEROLE

6 slices firm white bread,
  crust removed
4 T. melted butter or
  margarine
1 C. grated Swiss cheese
2 green onions, chopped
2 T. minced parsley

½ lb. small cooked shrimp
3 eggs
½ tsp. salt
½ tsp. mustard
1½ C. half and half
½ C. sour cream

Cut each slice of bread on diagonal and dip in melted butter or oleo. Arrange half of slices on bottom of 8" square ungreased casserole. Sprinkle with half of the cheese, onions, parsley and shrimp. Add remaining bread and repeat process. Beat eggs, salt, mustard, milk and sour cream together. Pour over casserole evenly. Cover and chill overnight. Bake, uncovered, at 350° for 30 to 40 minutes (until puffed and golden). Cut into squares. Garnish with cherry tomatoes and sprigs of fresh parsley. Serves 6 to 8.

SHRIMP STROGANOFF

2 lbs. shrimp, cooked
1 pt. sour cream
½ C. sliced black ripe
  olives
1 can cream of mushroom
  soup

1-8 oz. bag stroganoff
  noodles
1 T. dill weed
1 bunch green onions,
  chopped
1 C. sharp Cheddar cheese

Mix all together. Put in casserole dish. Top with 1 cup grated sharp Cheddar cheese and bake at 375° for 25 minutes until cheese is melted.

LAKE TROUT PARMESAN AU GRATIN

4 lake trout, cleaned
  (4 lbs. fish)
Juice of 1 lemon
3 egg yolks, beaten
2 T. butter, melted

1 pt. white sauce
½ C. Parmesan cheese
Salt and pepper
Parsley

Cut fish into serving portions, season with lemon juice, salt, pepper and butter; cover and bake until O done. Whip egg yolks and add to white sauce, add ½ of the cheese. Mask fish with this sauce, sprinkle with remaining cheese and dot with butter, bake until browned. Garnish with parsley.

TUNA CHOPSTICK

1 can cream of mushroom
  soup
¼ C. water
2 C. Chinese noodles (thin)
¼ C. onion

7 oz. can tuna
1 C. celery
Pepper to taste

Combine all ingredients and bake at 350° for 1 hour.

TUNA CASSEROLE

1 can tuna, drained   1½ T. butter
1 pkg. egg noodles, wide   1 T. flour
1 can chicken noodle soup   1 C. milk
5 oz. grated Cheddar cheese   Potato chips

Cook noodles as directed; drain well. Make sauce by cooking over medium heat. Cook butter and flour until frothy. Add milk, tuna and soup. Stir in cheese. Stir until cheese melts, lowering heat so it doesn't separate. Arrange noodles in oiled casserole and pour sauce over top. Crumble potato chips on top. Bake until chips are browned and casserole is bubbly.

OVERLANDER'S TUNA

¼ C. butter
¼ C. flour
2 C. milk
½ tsp. salt
1 C. grated Velveeta cheese
⅓ C. stuffed sliced green olives

Minced green pepper (optional)
1 C. flaked tuna
Cubed soft bread
Crushed corn flakes
Parmesan cheese

Combine butter, flour, milk and salt and make a white sauce. Add cheese, olives, pepper and tuna. Butter a 9x9" casserole and put cubed bread on the bottom. Pour tuna mixture over bread and top with crushed corn flakes and Parmesan cheese. Serves 4.

SEAFOOD CASSEROLE

2-10 oz. pkgs. frozen cream
  of shrimp soup
2 C. potato chips, crushed
2 C. chopped celery

2 tsp. Worcestershire sauce
½ C. mayonnaise
2 cans tuna fish
1 C. chopped onion

Mix soup and mayonnaise. Add 1½ cups potato chips along with rest of ingredients. Mix well. Sprinkle rest of chips on top. Bake at 350° for 30 minutes.

FISH AU GRATIN

1½ lbs. fish fillets
2 T. chopped onion
2 T. chopped celery

2 T. lemon juice
2 T. water
Salt and pepper
1 C. cheese sauce

Place fillets in 12x7" shallow baking pan. Sprinkle with onion and celery. Add water and lemon juice. Bake at 450° for 10 minutes. Remove from oven and pour cheese sauce over fish. Return to oven and continue baking for 10 to 15 minutes. Serves 4.

BAKED, BOILED & FRIED

BASS IN CREAM

2 lbs. dressed bass
¼ tsp. paprika
½ C. flour
¼ tsp. white pepper
1 tsp. salt

1 egg
1 T. water
¼ C. shortening
2 medium onions, sliced
½ C. cream

Dip fish in flour mixed with salt, pepper and paprika, then in egg beaten in water. Fry fish until brown on one side, then on the other. Place onions on top of fish. Cook until underside is brown. Drain fat. Pour cream over fish and if using dill, sprinkle over. Cover and simmer until cream is absorbed. For casserole variation: After frying fish, carefully place fish in casserole, pour cream over and if using dill, sprinkle over. Bake in 425° oven about 15 minutes. Serve with lemon wedges and garnish with parsley.

BAKED BASS WITH BACON

6 bass, cleaned
½ C. cornmeal
1 ½ tsp. salt
¼ tsp. paprika

1 T. flour
6 slices bacon
Pepper to taste

Clean and wash bass, drain. Mix flour, cornmeal, salt, pepper and paprika. Dip fish in cornmeal mixture. Place in single layer in a greased baking dish. Top with bacon. Bake at 425° for 20 minutes, or until fish is tender and bacon browned. (Onions may be baked around the fish, sliced thin.)

BAKED CARP

4 to 5 lbs. carp
1 onion, sliced
1 carrots, diced
½ C. celery
1 C. tomatoes

1 green pepper, chopped
½ C. margarine
⅓ C. flour
Salt and pepper
Paprika

In greased 9x13x2" baking dish, place all chopped vegetables on bottom. Dredge carp in flour, place carp on top of vegetables, sprinkle with salt and pepper. Drizzle melted margarine over carp, sprinkle with paprika. Bake in 375° oven 40 minutes; baste with its juice every 10 minutes. Serves 6 to 8.

SPICY CARP

3 lbs. sliced carp	1 ¼ C. warm water
5 gingersnaps	½ tsp. whole pickling spice
2 onions, sliced	¼ tsp. salt
¼ C. oil	1 T. lemon juice
2 carrots, sliced	⅛ tsp. white pepper

Pour ½ oil in baking dish, arrange half of fish on top; cover with ½ of sliced onion and carrots, add remaining fish and vegetables. Soften gingersnaps in water and lemon juice and stir until softened and smooth. Add spices, salt and white pepper; pour over fish. Add remaining oil and more water, if necessary, to cover fish. Cover dish and bake at 325° for 1 hour. Serves 4.

BOILED CARP

Dress fish. Rub with salt and wrap in cheesecloth. Tie ends and place in kettle of water. Add 1 teaspoon salt, slices of onions, sprig of parsley, 1 tablespoon lemon or vinegar, 1 bay leaf. Simmer 10 minutes to the pound.

CATFISH PARMESAN

6 skinned, pan-dressed
  catfish, fresh or frozen
1 C. dry bread crumbs
¾ C. grated Parmesan
  cheese
¼ C. chopped parsley
1 tsp. paprika
½ tsp. whole oregano

¼ tsp. whole basil
2 tsp. salt
½ tsp. pepper
½ C. melted butter or
  margarine
Lemon wedges
Parsley

Pat fish dry. Combine bread crumbs, Parmesan cheese and seasonings; stir well. Dip catfish in butter and roll each in crumbs mixture. Arrange fish in a well-greased 13x9x2" baking dish. Bake at 375° about 25 minutes or until fish flakes easily when tested with a fork. Garnish with lemon wedges and parsley. Serves 6.

HERB BAKED FISH

½ C. butter or margarine
⅔ C. crushed saltine
  crackers
¼ C. grated Parmesan
  cheese
½ tsp. salt

½ tsp. basil leaves
½ tsp. oregano leaves
¼ tsp. garlic powder
1 lb. frozen codfish fillets,
  thawed and drained

Preheat oven to 350°. Melt butter in a 13x9" baking pan. Combine cracker crumbs, Parmesan cheese, basil, oregano, salt and garlic powder in a 9" pie pan. Dip fish fillets in butter and then in crumb mixture. Arrange in baking pan. Bake for 25 to 30 minutes. Serve immediately. Serves 4.

BAKED BROCCOLI FISH

1 lb. flounder or lemon sole
  fillets
1 can cream of celery soup

1 pkg. frozen (or fresh)
  broccoli spears
3 T. milk
Pepper to taste

Take strips of fish, roll around broccoli spear. Place rolled fish pieces into oblong or Pyrex or tin pan. Stir milk into soup. Pour mixture over fish. Add pepper to taste. Cover tin and bake at 375° for 40 minutes. Uncover for remaining 5 to 10 minutes. May serve with lemon slices. Enjoy! Serves 2 to 3.

BAKED FLOUNDER VINAIGRETTE

1 lb. flounder fillets
3 T. Italian (reduced-calorie)
  salad dressing
Paprika

1 large tomato, sliced thin
1 T. minced chives
¼ C. (1 oz.) shredded
  Cheddar cheese

Arrange fillets in a shallow baking dish; brush salad dressing over fillets; sprinkle with chives. Bake, uncovered, at 450° for 10 minutes. Sprinkle with cheese and bake an additional 2 to 3 minutes, or until fillets flake with a fork. Serves 4.

BAKED HALIBUT

2 large halibut steaks,
  ½" thick
1 tsp. salt
¼ C. milk

1 C. crushed corn flakes
2 T. melted butter
Paprika

Dip steaks in salted milk, then in the crushed corn flakes to coat thoroughly on both sides. Place on greased baking sheet. Drizzle tops of steaks with melted butter. Add dash of paprika. Bake in hot oven, 500 to 550° for 10 to 15 minutes.

HALIBUT BE THY NAME

1 can mushroom soup
2 pkgs. frozen or equivalent
  of fresh halibut, sole, or
  flounder

1 large onion
6 oz. grated Cheddar
  cheese

Spread ½ can of soup on bottom of casserole. Add the fish. Spread onions and cheese on top of fish. Cover with remaining soup. Sprinkle with bread crumbs. Bake at 325° for 45 minutes. Serve with green salad or fruit salad.

ORANGE ROUGHY FISH FILLETS WITH PINEAPPLE

1½ lbs. orange roughy fish
  fillets or snappers
Salt to taste
1 onion
2 T. oil
1 T. brown sugar

2 T. cornstarch
¼ C. vinegar or lemon juice
1 tsp. ground ginger
1 T. soy sauce
1 C. pineapple pieces and
  juice

Cut fish into serving-size pieces and rub with salt. Place in 2- to 3-quart casserole. Peel and slice onion and saute in hot oil in pan. Mix all other ingredients and pour into pan, stirring until mixture thickens. Pour sauce over fish in casserole. Cover and bake at 350° for about 30 minutes. Serve with boiled rice. Serves 4.

SAUTEED PRAWN WITH TOMATO SAUCE

12 fresh prawn (2 lbs.)
10 T. oil
3 T. catsup
2 tsp. salt
¼ tsp. pepper
2 T. Worcestershire

2 C. onions, shredded
1 T. wine
1 T. sugar
½ C. water
¼ tsp. sesame oil
1 T. cornstarch + 1 T. water
  (make paste)

Cut each prawn down the back and dry. Stir-fry the shredded onion with 3 tablespoons oil until soft. Season with ½ teaspoon of salt. Remove to a platter. Heat 5 tablespoons oil in a pan, put in the prawns, shake pan to evenly cook. When red, turn them over and fry the other side until completely done. (One minute on each side on low heat.) Sprinkle with 1 tablespoon wine, then remove. Heat another 2 tablespoons oil in same pan. Add catsup and pour in sugar, salt, water, pepper, sesame oil and Worcestershire sauce and bring to a boil. Then put fried prawns back into sauce. Stir-fry 1 minute. Thicken the sauce with cornstarch paste. Place on platter over the fried onions and serve.

LAHAINA RED SNAPPER

2 lbs. skinless red snapper
   fillets
2 T. olive oil
1½ C. thinly sliced onions
2 C. mixed, sliced red and
   green peppers
1 T. chopped garlic
1 C. sliced celery

2 C. chopped ripe tomatoes
¼ C. drained capers
¼ C. chopped fresh parsley
½ tsp. salt
Fresh ground black pepper
¼ tsp. Tabasco sauce
2 T. butter

Cut fish into 6 portions. Heat olive oil in a saucepan and add onions, peppers, garlic and celery. Cook, stirring, for about 5 minutes. Add the tomatoes to pan along with capers, parsley, salt, pepper and Tabasco. Cover pan and cook for 10 minutes. Put fish in a 9x13" baking dish. Spoon sauce over fish and dot with butter. Place the baking dish on top of stove and bring sauce to boil. Place dish in 425° oven and bake for 12 minutes. Serves 6.

VIRGINIA BAKED SCALLOPS

1 lb. scallops
¼ C. sliced onions
2 T. cooking oil
1 can condensed shrimp
  soup
4 T. sour cream
3 T. white wine

10 oz. asparagus spears,
  cooked, cut and drained
1 T. lemon juice
2 C. coarsely broken potato
  chips
16 to 20 whole potato chips

Rinse scallops with cold water and dry. Cook scallops and onion in skillet with oil about 5 minutes or until scallops are tender. Add soup, sour cream and wine. Blend well. Fold in asparagus and lemon juice; heat. Sprinkle broken potato chips over bottom of a shallow 1½-quart baking dish. Spoon half of scallop mixture over crushed potato chips. Stand whole potato chips upon end around edge of fish. Add remaining scallop mixture. Bake in 400° oven for 10 to 12 minutes or until bubbly and hot in center.

SHRIMP SCAMPI

2½ lbs. fresh shrimp
½ C. onions, wedges
½ C. celery, sliced
½ C. bell peppers, sliced
1 C. butter, melted
¼ C. olive oil
1 T. fresh parsley or dried
  flakes

1 T. lemon juice
¾ tsp. salt
¾ tsp. garlic powder
¾ tsp. dried whole basil
½ tsp. dried oregano
Hot rice

Peel and devein shrimp. Place these in a single layer in a jellyroll pan. Meanwhile, saute the onions, celery and bell peppers in a skillet. Place over the shrimp, set aside. Combine the melted butter, olive oil, parsley, lemon juice, salt, garlic powder, basil and oregano; pour over the shrimp and vegetables. Bake at 450° for 5 minutes, then broil 4" from heat for 5 minutes or until done. Serve over a bed of hot, cooked rice. Serves about 6.

SWEET AND SOUR SHRIMP

SAUCE:
1 C. stock
1 C. pineapple syrup
½ C. white vinegar
2 T. soy sauce
4 T. brown sugar

3 T. water
2 T. cornstarch
1 large green pepper
2 to 3 tomatoes
4 to 6 slices of pineapple

Heat stock, syrup, vinegar, soy sauce and brown sugar. When boiling, add paste of water and cornstarch. Cook until thick. Add vegetables to sauce but do not cook further. Combine sauce and Butterfly Shrimp.

BUTTERFLY SHRIMP:

2 lbs. large shrimp
½ C. flour
1 T. cornstarch
2 T. water
½ tsp. MSG
1 large egg, beaten
1 tsp. salt
1 tsp. baking powder

Combine flour, cornstarch, salt, baking powder and MSG with water and beaten egg. Dip shrimp in batter and fry in oil to light brown.

BAKED SHRIMP

2 lbs. large shrimp
  (about 32), shelled
  and deveined, tails left
  intact if you wish
1 C. (2 sticks) butter, melted
¼ C. dry white wine
¼ C. minced parsley

2 T. fresh lemon juice
3 large cloves minced garlic
2 tsp. basil
1 tsp. Worcestershire sauce
¾ to 1 tsp. hot pepper sauce
½ tsp. salt
½ C. dry, unseasoned bread
  crumbs

Preheat oven to 450°. Combine all ingredients except shrimp and bread crumbs in a shallow 2-quart baking dish and mix well. Remove ¼ cup of this mixture and set aside. Add shrimp to baking dish and coat thoroughly. Combine bread crumbs with reserved butter sauce and sprinkle over shrimp. Bake 10 to 15 minutes. Serve immediately. Serves 6 to 8.

LOUISIANA BARBECUED SHRIMP

1 C. butter
1 C. vegetable oil
2 tsp. minced garlic
4 whole bay leaves, crushed
  fine
2 tsp. crushed dried rosemary
  leaves
½ tsp. dried basil
½ tsp. oregano

½ tsp. salt
½ tsp. cayenne pepper
1 T. paprika
¾ tsp. fresh ground black
  pepper
1 tsp. lemon juice
2 lbs. whole, fresh shrimp in
  the shell

In saucepan, melt butter. Add vegetable oil and mix. Add all other ingredients except shrimp. Cook over medium heat, stirring, until mixture begins to boil. Reduce heat to low and cook for 7 to 8 minutes, stirring frequently. Remove from heat, let stand, uncovered, for 30 minutes at room temperature. Add shrimp to mixture. Put back on medium heat for 6 to 8 minutes or just until shrimp turns pink. Transfer to baking dish or casserole and bake at 450° for 10 minutes. To serve, ladle generous portion of sauce over each portion of shrimp. Serve in individual ramekins or soup bowls.

SHRIMP DE JONGHE

⅔ C. butter
2 T. chives
½ tsp. garlic powder

⅛ tsp. pepper
2-10 oz. pkgs. frozen cocktail
   size shrimp, thawed and
   drained
1½ C. thin bacon flavored
   crackers, crushed

In heavy 2-quart saucepan, melt butter over medium heat. Stir in chives, garlic powder and pepper. Dip shrimp in this mixture and then roll in cracker crumbs. Layer shrimp in 8" square baking dish. Add remaining cracker crumbs to mixture, stir and sprinkle over shrimp. Bake at 350° for 25 to 30 minutes or until shrimp is tender. Serves 4.

SHRIMP COOKED IN BEER

Shrimp   Salt
Beer

Wash shrimp, put in pan and just cover with beer. Add salt and let come to a boil. Time them and boil for 10 minutes with lid on. Watch so they don't boil over. Very good with cocktail sauce and crackers.

CHINESE SHRIMP AND VEGETABLES

7 oz. (small) box Minute rice
1 pkg. frozen Chinese
  vegetables (do not use
  flavor packet)
8 oz. frozen shrimp

3 small onions, chopped
1 green pepper, chopped
½ C. chopped celery
2 T. butter
2 T. Worcestershire sauce
1 chopped tomato

Cook each of the first 3 ingredients as directed on package. Combine the second 3 ingredients and saute in 2 tablespoons butter and Worcestershire sauce. Combine all ingredients. Add chopped tomato and stir with 2 or more tablespoons of soy sauce.

CHIPPER TROUT

2 lbs. fish fillets
½ C. Caesar's salad
  dressing

1 C. crushed potato chips
½ C. sharp Cheddar cheese

Dip fish in salad dressing and place skin-side down in shallow pan. Combine chips and cheese and sprinkle on fish. Bake at 375° for 15 to 20 minutes or until fish is light and flaky.

SAGED TROUT

3 brook trout (1 lb.)	Salt
2 leaves sage	White pepper
⅓ C. flour	1/16 tsp. nutmeg
5½ T. butter	

Split trout on stomach side, remove bones, wash and dry with towel. Sprinkle with salt and roll in flour. Brown in 3 tablespoons butter, fry, stomach down 5 minutes. Turn and fry on other side. Place on platter. Melt remaining butter and crush sage, add nutmeg; pour over fish. Garnish with lemon wedges. Serves 3.

TROUT BAKED WITH WINE

½ C. dry white wine
1 tsp. dried tarragon leaves
8 trout, about 5 to 6 oz. each
  (other fish may be used)
4 tsp. lemon juice

Salt to taste
White pepper
¼ C. melted butter
½ tsp. chopped parsley

Heat oven to 375°. Brush inside of fish with salt, pepper and melted butter. Sprinkle with lemon juice, tarragon, salt and white pepper on outside. Pour wine around fish. Cover and bake 15 minutes or until flaky. Serve with garnish of chopped parsley. Serves 4.

WRAPPED TROUT

*6 brook trout (may use
   other small fish)*

*12 slices bacon
Seasonings*

Clean, scale and drain fish. Rinse in clean water and drain. Season inside with salt and pepper (try lemon-pepper). Wrap each fish in 2 strips of bacon and fasten with toothpicks or metal skewers. Broil slowly over charcoals or in a stove broiler. When bacon is dark and crisp, fish will be done. Serves 6.

BRAZILIAN BAKED TROUT

4 to 6 medium trout (½ lb. each)
1 tsp. salt
1 C. white wine
2 T. green onion rings

4 T. melted butter
1 lemon
1 clove garlic
2 T. chopped parsley
2 T. dry bread crumbs

Wash and dry 4 to 6 medium trout (½ pound each); rub outsides with lemon juice (1 lemon). Sprinkle with salt (1 teaspoon). Arrange minced garlic in bottom of buttered, shallow baking dish. Place trout in single layer and pour white wine over top. Sprinkle with 2 tablespoons each chopped parsley, green onion rings and dry bread crumbs and 4 tablespoons melted butter. Bake in 400° oven for 20 minutes. Serves 4 to 6.

BAKED TROUT

6 trout, about the same size
1 tsp. chopped parsley
1 onion, chopped fine
3 oz. raw mushrooms,
  chopped fine
½ tsp. tarragon leaves
2 T. melted butter

SAUCE FOR BAKING:
4 egg yolks
3 T. brandy
⅛ tsp. white pepper
½ C. bread crumbs
½ C. grated Swiss cheese
⅛ tsp. paprika

Grease a 9x13x2" baking dish. Spread with mixture of parsley, onion, mushrooms, salt and pepper. Arrange trout on vegetables and sprinkle with tarragon and melted butter. Cover with foil and bake in 400° oven for 10 minutes. Mix together egg yolks, brandy, salt and white pepper. Remove foil from trout. Pour egg mixture over fish and sprinkle with mixture of crumbs and Swiss cheese. Sprinkle top with paprika and return to oven until crumbs are browned. Delicious with grilled tomatoes, onions and mushrooms as side dish. Serves 6.

TROUT STUFFED
(JAPANESE STYLE)

½ lb. mushrooms, sliced
1 C. peppers, cut in strips
3 scallions, sliced with
  greens
1 C. bean sprouts
2 stalks celery, sliced
  ½" thick diagonally

2 T. vegetable oil
4 eggs, lightly beaten
2 tsp. soy sauce
4 trout 8 to 10 oz., boned
  with skin, head and tail on
8 strips bacon

Mix vegetables together. In a large skillet or wok, heat oil, then toss in the vegetables and stir-fry for 2 minutes. Add the eggs and soy sauce and continue to toss and cook for another minute until eggs begin to coagulate. Stuff each of the trout with ¼ of the vegetable mixture; the filling will expand the opening about an inch. Wrap 2 slices of bacon around each trout. Tuck the ends underneath. Place in large baking pan so they do not touch. Bake in preheated 400° oven about 15 minutes until skin is crisp and the fish opaque to the bone. Test after 12 minutes. Vegetables will remain crisp.

FRIED TURTLE AND ONIONS

1 turtle, cut in serving pieces
½ C. flour
3 T. oil
1 tsp. salt

½ tsp. caraway seed
3 to 4 onions, sliced
1 clove garlic, crushed
 (if desired)
Pepper to taste

Dredge the turtle in seasoned flour. Fry to brown on all sides in hot oil. Sprinkle with caraway seeds, onion and garlic. Add 1 cup of water; cover and simmer for 1 hour or until tender and water has cooked away. Cooking time may vary according to age of turtle.

TURTLE A LA KING

2 C. cooked turtle
2 C. half and half
2 T. butter
1 tsp. flour

6 yolks of hard-cooked eggs
⅛ tsp. nutmeg
⅛ tsp. allspice
Salt and pepper to taste

Mash hard-cooked egg yolks with the butter and flour. In double boiler, heat half and half to scald; stir in egg mixture and stir until smooth. Add the seasonings. Add the turtle and simmer for 10 minutes. Serve hot.

FISH BAKED IN WINE

Any white fish, sole, halibut, sea bass, large catfish, etc. or salmon is good prepared this way.

2 lbs. fish fillets or slices
Salt and pepper
1 large onion, sliced
1 C. white table wine
  (sauterne or Chablis)

3 T. butter or margarine
2 fresh tomatoes , sliced or
  1-8 oz. can tomato sauce
½ green pepper, sliced
2 tsp. Worcestershire sauce

Sprinkle fish with salt and pepper; cover with sliced onion. Pour wine over all and let stand 30 minutes. Melt butter in large shallow baking pan; remove fish and onion from wine and place in pan. Cover with tomatoes and green pepper. Sprinkle with salt. Bake in moderately hot oven (375°) about 35 minutes or until fish is tender, basting frequently with a mixture of the wine in which the fish was soaked and the Worcestershire sauce. Serves 6.

FISH AND CHIPS
(SCOTCH)

½ lb. fresh or frozen fish
  fillets
1 large or 2 small baking
  potatoes, peeled
2 T. flour
¼ tsp. salt
1 T. water

1 tsp. cooking oil
1 egg yolk
1 stiff-beaten egg white
Fat for deep fat frying
2 T. flour
Malt vinegar (optional)

Thaw fish, if frozen. Cut fish into 2 serving-size pieces. Pat dry with paper towel. Cut potatoes lengthwise into ⅜" wide strips. For batter, in mixing bowl, stir together 2 tablespoons flour and ¼ teaspoon salt. Add water, oil and egg yolk; beat until smooth. Fold in stiff-beaten egg white. Fry potato strips in hot fat for 5 or 6 minutes or until golden brown. Remove and drain on towel and sprinkle with salt. Cover with foil to keep warm. Coat fish pieces evenly with 2 tablespoons flour, then dip in batter. Fry in hot fat for 2 to 2H minutes on each side or until golden. Remove and drain on paper towel. Serve fish with malt vinegar drizzled on it and with fried potatoes.

SWEET AND SOUR FISH

1 lb. fish fillets
1 tsp. sherry
2 tsp. salt
½ tsp. white pepper
3 egg whites
3 T. cornstarch

SAUCE:
6 T. white vinegar
6 T. sugar
2 tsp. soy sauce
4 T. water
½ tsp. salt
1 tsp. minced fresh ginger
1 T. cornstarch (make thin
   paste with water)
1 green pepper, diced

Cut fish fillets into pieces 2x1". Season with salt, pepper and sherry. Beat egg whites with cornstarch until foamy, not stiff. Dip each piece of fish in egg whites and refrigerate 1 hour. Heat oil in wok or frypan. Deep-fry for about 2 minutes or until done. Place in oven, uncovered, to keep warm. Place on paper towels to drain.

SAUCE: Cook vinegar, water, sugar, salt, ginger and soy sauce. Bring to boil. Stir in cornstarch mixture and cook until sauce thickens. Add green pepper. Pour over fish and serve at once. Sauce can be prepared ahead of time and refrigerated. Serves 3.

BARBECUED FISH

1-8 oz. can tomato sauce
2 lbs. fish fillets or
 pan-sized fish
2 T. chopped onion
2 T. lemon juice
1 T. Worcestershire sauce
2 T. chopped green pepper

1 clove garlic, minced fine
2 T. melted butter
1 T. brown sugar
2 tsp. salt
½ tsp. chili powder
2 T. lemon juice

Clean and scale fish. Cook onion, green pepper and garlic in fat until tender. Add remaining ingredients and simmer for 5 minutes, stirring occasionally. Cool. Cut fish into serving portions. Place fish in a single layer in a shallow baking dish. Pour sauce over fish and let stand for 30 minutes; turning once. Remove fish, reserving sauce for basting. Place fish in well-greased, hinged, wire grills. Cook about 4" from moderately hot coals for 5 to 8 minutes. Baste with sauce. Turn and grill 5 to 8 more minutes, until fish is tender and flaky. You may do fish the same way in stove broiler. Serves 6.

RAINBOW RIVER BARGE FISH DISH

Fish fillets (any kind)
White wine
1 diced onion

1 C. mayonnaise
1 C. sour cream
Bread crumbs

Soak fish fillets in white wine for 4 to 8 hours. Pat dry and drain well. Mix in sour cream and mayonnaise well. Add onion to mixture. Place one half of mixture in shallow baking dish large enough to hold fillets. Roll fish in bread crumbs and lay on top of mixture. Cover fish with remaining mixture and top with bread crumbs. Bake at 450° for 10 minutes.

BAKED FISH WITH SOUR CREAM

3 lbs. fresh fish (use your
   favorite)
6 strips bacon
2 T. oil or butter
Salt and pepper
1 T. chopped parsley

1 C. sour cream
½ C. Parmesan cheese
⅓ C. buttered crumbs
1 T. lemon juice
1 T. Parmesan cheese

Lay fish on strips of bacon, after having rubbed them with salt, pepper and oil or butter, in shallow baking dish. Make mixture of sour cream, Parmesan cheese, crumbs and lemon juice and spread it over the fish. Bake at 350° for 40 minutes until tender. Sprinkle with grated cheese and parsley. Serves 6.

PICKLED FISH

Clean and cut fish in 1" wide pieces. Soak 24 hours in brine of pickling salt and water strong enough to float an egg. Drain, then soak fish in white vinegar for 24 hours. Drain and discard vinegar. Mix 1 cup sugar, 1 cup water and 2 cups white vinegar. Boil 5 minutes and cool. Add 1 cup of white wine (Silver Satin) and 3 tablespoons of pickling spices. At this time remove skin and all visible bones and backbone. Put fish in jar. For each 3 pounds of fish, add 3 cups sliced onions. Pour cool brine solution over fish and onions and let stand at least 3 days in refrigerator before eating. Most all fish may be prepared this way.

DEEP FAT FRIED FISH

2 lbs. fish fillets
1½ C. dry bread crumbs, or
  use cracker crumbs
1 egg, beaten

¾ tsp. salt
Pepper to taste
¼ C. milk
Fat for frying

Cut fish in serving portions. Combine milk, egg, salt and pepper. Dip fish in milk and roll in crumbs. Place in a single layer in the fryer basket. Fry in deep fat, 350°, for 4 to 5 minutes or until brown and flakes. Drain on absorbent paper. Serves 6.

FAST FIXIN' FISH

2 T. butter or margarine
1 env. Lipton golden
  mushroom soup mix

1 T. chopped parsley
¾ C. water
1 lb. fish fillets

In medium skillet, melt butter; stir in soup mix and parsley blended with water. Add fish, simmer (covered) 10 minutes or until fish flakes. Serves 4.

POACHED FISH

¾ lb. fillets
½ C. orange juice

1 small orange
1 tsp. parsley, minced

In a large skillet, poach fish by placing fillets in skillet and covering with orange juice. Heat and cook until nearly cooked through, then turn to finish cooking by placing peeled, sectioned orange over fillets. Cover skillet and simmer slowly until cooked. Sprinkle with parsley and serve over cooked rice.

STUFFED FISH MAGNIFIQUE

1 lb. fish fillets (4 fillets)
1-7 oz. can crabmeat
½ C. shredded Swiss or
  Jack cheese

2 T. parsley, snipped
¼ C. seasoned Italian bread
  crumbs

Drain, flake and remove cartilage from crabmeat. Place in a bowl and mix together with cheese, parsley and bread crumbs. Spread filling lengthwise over fillets. Fold fillets over filling and secure with toothpick. Place fillets seam side down in a lightly-greased glass 9x13" casserole dish. Sprinkle with a little melted butter and more bread crumbs. Bake in a 400° oven for about 20 to 30 minutes. Don't overcook fish or it will dry out.

GEFILTE FISH

1 jar gefilte fish (6 or 8
   pieces without liquid)
2 grated carrots
¼ C. bread crumbs or
   matzo meal

¼ C. margarine
1 egg
1 T. parsley flakes

Mash all ingredients and mix together. Put into any size pan. Sprinkle with paprika. Bake at 350° for 30 to 40 minutes.

ITALIAN SAUCED FISH

1-1 lb. pkg. frozen fillets
1-4 oz. can spaghetti sauce

1 T. chopped onion
2 oz. shredded mozzarella
cheese

Arrange fillets in baking dish. Top with onion and sauce. Sprinkle with cheese. Cover and bake at 350° for 25 minutes. Serves 4.

SICILIAN SARDINE
(SMELT)

1 pkg. smelt
½ C. flour
Salt and pepper to taste

½ C. vinegar
¼ C. olive oil
3 cloves garlic

Dip the smelt in flour. Have olive oil hot in a frypan. Turn heat to medium and fry the smelt on both sides. When done, add the garlic, squashed. Add the vinegar, cook for 2 to 3 minutes; salt and pepper to taste.

FROG LEGS

Large (jumbo) and small frog legs are available. Allow 4 to 6 large legs or 8 to 12 small legs per serving. When purchased in the market, the legs are skinned, cleaned and ready to cook. When you catch your own, use only the hind legs, cut off close to body. Wash and pull off skin from top to bottom. To avoid the muscle contractions which may continue in fresh frog legs during preparation and cooking, the legs may be thoroughly chilled before cooking.

FRIED FROG LEGS: Wash frog legs; dry thoroughly. Sprinkle with salt and pepper. Dip in flour or egg and crumbs. Place in ¼ to ½" of heated fat (preferably part or all butter). Cook until browned, turning to brown on both sides. Serve with Lemon Butter.

LEMON BUTTER: Combine 2 to 3 tablespoons lemon juice with ½ cup creamed or melted butter.

MISCELLANEOUS

SPICY CRAB SALAD

1 lb. backfin or regular
  crabmeat
1 medium onion, chopped
4 T. mayonnaise, rounded

2 T. mustard
1 tsp. Worcestershire sauce
¼ tsp. seafood seasoning
Salt to taste

Toss crabmeat and onion. Mix mayonnaise, mustard, Worcestershire and seafood seasoning together and add to crabmeat; toss lightly. Refrigerate at least 1 hour before serving.

SUMMER TUNA MAC SALAD

8 oz. macaroni, cooked
1 can tuna, flaked and drained
1 C. celery, diced

½ C. onion, diced
Salt and pepper to taste
½ C. mayonnaise
1 tsp. lemon juice

Combine all ingredients except macaroni. Toss with macaroni; chill.

SHRIMP SALAD

1 lb. shrimp, medium,
  coarsely cut
¼ C. mustard

½ C. stuffed olives, halved
  or sliced
½ C. green onions,
  including stems
½ to 1 tsp. mayonnaise

Mix thoroughly.

CRABMEAT QUICHE

8 oz. Swiss cheese, broken
  into pieces
2 T. flour
2 beaten eggs

½ C. milk
½ C. mayonnaise
4 chopped green onions
6 oz. crabmeat (shrimp or
  lobster)

Mix all ingredients, add dash of salt. Pour into 9", deep-dish pie pan shell.
Bake at 400° for 5 minutes, reduce heat and bake at 300° until puffed and
brown, approximately 35 minutes. Serves 6.

TUNA QUICHE

1 can tuna, drained
¼ lb. yellow cheese
   (muenster or Cheddar)
¼ lb. mushrooms
2 medium onions

3 T. oil
2 T. mayonnaise
2 T. sour cream
½ tsp. paprika
¼ tsp. Tabasco sauce

Chop onion, saute in oil until soft. Add mushrooms. Combine tuna with the grated cheese, mayonnaise, sour cream, paprika, Tabasco and sauteed onion and mushrooms. Put into 10" ready-made or homemade pie shell. Cover with another layer of dough and flute sides. Bake at 350° for 40 minutes.

BUTTER TOAST CUPS WITH TUNA

6 slices day-old bread
3 T. soft margarine
¼ C. chopped onion
4 T. butter
3 T. flour
1 tsp. salt

¼ tsp. pepper
2 C. milk
1 C. canned English peas
1-7 oz. can tuna fish
3 T. chopped pimento
¼ C. grated Cheddar
  cheese

Remove crusts from bread; butter both sides of bread. Press into muffin tins and toast in moderate oven until golden brown. Cook onion in butter until golden, stir in flour and blend. Add salt and pepper. Gradually add milk and cook over low heat until thickened, stirring constantly. Stir in remaining ingredients and heat until cheese melts. Serve in the toast cups. Serves 6.

HOT TUNA BUNS

1-7 oz. can white tuna
4 stuffed, green olives
4 oz. Cheddar cheese cubes
3 hard-cooked eggs, sliced

2 T. chopped onions
¼ tsp. salt
⅓ C. mayonnaise
3 T. sweet pickle relish
8 hot dog or hamburger
   buns

Drain and flake tuna and combine with all other ingredients. Spoon into sliced buns. Wrap individually in foil. Bake 10 minutes on cookie sheet at 400°. Serve in foil.

TUNA ROLL

2 C. flour
1 T. and 1 tsp. baking powder
1 tsp. salt
¼ C. shortening
¾ C. milk
1 egg, beaten
1-7 oz. can tuna, drained
  and flaked

1½ T. chopped parsley
2 tsp. grated onion
¼ C. sweet pickle relish
CHEESE SAUCE:
3 T. butter
2 T. flour
1½ C. milk
½ C. shredded Cheddar
  cheese

Mix flour, baking powder and salt. Cut in shortening. Add ½ cup milk and egg. Combine ingredients thoroughly. Knead dough on floured surface a few times. Roll out into a rectangle 14x12x¼". Preheat oven. Combine tuna, parsley, onion, ¼ cup milk and salt. Add pickle relish. Mix well. Spread mixture onto dough. Roll dough as for a jellyroll. Place seam-side down on a greased cookie sheet. Bake for about 40 minutes. Make cheese sauce by combining butter, flour and milk and heating. Then add cheese and stir until cheese is melted. Slice Tuna Roll and serve hot with Cheese Sauce topping.

SHRIMP TURNOVERS

½ lb. cooked shrimp
1 tsp. horseradish
2 T. lemon juice
1 tsp. prepared mustard
Cream

1 T. chopped sweet pickles
1 tsp. salt
3 tsp. mayonnaise
1 C. pastry mix

Grind shrimp. Combine all ingredients, except pastry mix and cream, blend into a paste. Prepare pastry as directed. Roll very thin and cut into 2" circles. Place teaspoon of filling in center of each circle. Moisten edges with cold water, fold over and press edges together with a fork. Prick tops and brush with cream. Bake in hot oven, 475°, for 12 to 15 minutes or until golden brown. Makes about 48 turnovers.

SHRIMP FRIED RICE

1 large onion
1 large bell pepper
1 tsp. soy sauce
½ stick butter

1 lb. cleaned shrimp
2 C. cooked rice
2 eggs

Chop onion and bell pepper and cook in butter in an iron skillet. Do not brown. Add shrimp and soy sauce and cook until shrimp are pink. Salt and pepper to taste. Pull shrimp to side of pan, leaving center clean. Add 1 tablespoon cooking oil. Break 2 eggs in center and cook until done. Stir all ingredients together. Add rice and sprinkle soy sauce. Stir together and steam on low heat for 20 minutes. If rice is very dry, you might have to add ¼ cup water. Serves 4.

BEER BATTER

¾ C. flour
½ C. beer, flat, room
  temperature
1 egg
1 tsp. vegetable oil

Salt to taste
1 lb. fish fillets
2 T. vegetable oil (for frying)
Salt and pepper to taste

Combine first 5 ingredients. Cut fillets into 2" pieces. Heat oil for frying. Dip fish into batter and fry in hot oil for 4 to 5 minutes on each side. Drain on paper towels.

FISH BREADING

Dip fish or meat in mixture of 1 beaten egg and 2 tablespoons milk. Roll in 1 cup cornmeal blended with 2 teaspoons salt. Fry until browned.

UNI-Cookbook Categories

1100	Cookies	3400	Low Cholesterol
1200	Casseroles	3500	Chocoholic
1300	Meat Dishes	3700	Cajun
1400	Microwave	3800	Household Hints
1500	Cooking for "2"	6100	Chinese Recipes
1600	Slow Cooking	6400	German Recipes
1700	Low Calorie	6700	Italian Recipes
1900	Pastries & Pies	6800	Irish Recipes
2000	Charcoal Grilling	7000	Mexican Recipes
2100	Hors D'oeuvres	7100	Norwegian Recipes
2200	Beef	7200	Swedish Recipes
2300	Holiday Collections		
2400	Salads & Dressings		
2500	How to Cook Wild Game		
2600	Soups		
3100	Seafood & Fish		
3200	Poultry		
3300	My Own Recipes		

Available Titles 1/94

Titles change without notice.

G&R
Publishing Co.
507 Industrial Street
Waverly, IA 50677